This Journal Belongs to

Published by

Passion Life Publishing

Made in the USA
Middletown, DE
25 February 2020

85294033R00068